Leckie
the education publisher
for Scotland

Primary **Maths**
for Scotland

1st Level Maths

1C

Practice Workbook 1

© 2024 Leckie

001/01082024

10 9 8 7 6 5 4 3 2 1

ISBN 9780008680312

Published by
Leckie
An imprint of HarperCollins Publishers
Westerhill Road, Bishopbriggs, Glasgow, G64 2QT

T: 0844 576 8126 F: 0844 576 8131
leckiescotland@harpercollins.co.uk www.leckiescotland.co.uk

HarperCollins Publishers
Macken House, 39/40 Mayor Street Upper, Dublin 1, D01 C9W8, Ireland

Publisher: Fiona McGlade

Special thanks
Project editor: Peter Dennis
Layout: Siliconchips
Proofreader: Julianna Dunn

A CIP Catalogue record for this book is available from the British Library.

Acknowledgements
Images © Shutterstock.com

Printed in India by Multivista Global Pvt. Ltd.

Contents

Answers

Check your answers to this workbook online: https://collins.co.uk/pages/scottish-primary-maths

1 What is the nearest hundred to each number? Use the number lines to help you. Circle your answer.

a) 263

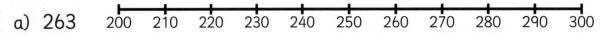

200 210 220 230 240 250 260 270 280 290 300

b) 653

600 610 620 630 640 650 660 670 680 690 700

c) 150

100 110 120 130 140 150 160 170 180 190 200

d) 981

900 910 920 930 940 950 960 970 980 990 1000

e) 847

800 810 820 830 840 850 860 870 880 890 900

f) 47

0 10 20 30 40 50 60 70 80 90 100

2 Isla's teacher has asked her to round these numbers to the nearest 100. Should Isla round UP or DOWN? Tick the correct answer.

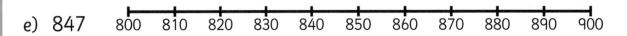

a) 33   UP   DOWN   b) 50   UP   DOWN

c) 510   UP   DOWN   d) 380   UP   DOWN

e) 950   UP   DOWN   f) 561   UP   DOWN

3 Round these numbers to the nearest 100.

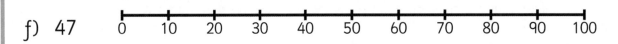

a) 360 ⬭   b) 340 ⬭   c) 350 ⬭

d) 550 ⬭   e) 523 ⬭   f) 573 ⬭

4 A café owner wants to know roughly how many customers visit his café on different days. Complete the table.

Customers visiting	Actual number	To the nearest 10	To the nearest 100
Monday	111		
Tuesday	264	260	
Wednesday	255		
Thursday	191		
Friday	377		
Saturday	491		
Sunday	342		

★ Challenge

Nuria thinks of a number.

When I round to the nearest 10 I get 220.
When I round to the nearest 100 I get 200.

Finlay says Nuria's number is 219. Isla says it is 225. Amman thinks it could be 222.

Whose answer is definitely incorrect? Why?

Write down all the possible numbers that Nuria could be thinking of.

1.2 Estimating the answer by rounding

1 Round each number to the nearest 100 to estimate the answer to each calculation. Circle the more reasonable estimate.

a) 121 + 383 is about 500
                        600

b) 51 + 629 is about 600
                     700

c) 328 + 555 is about 800
                      900

d) 690 + 232 is about 800
                      900

e) 789 + 189 is about 900
                      1000

f) 377 + 465 is about 800
                     900

2 Read these number problems. Use rounding to 10 to estimate the answers and check which ones are reasonable.

Write a new estimate for any that are unreasonable.

a) 49 + 93 is about 140

b) 51 + 193 is about 200

c) 212 + 36 is about 350

d) 142 + 46 is about 190

e) 18 + 58 is about 110

f) 162 + 142 is about 200

3 Read these number problems. Use rounding to 10 to estimate the answers and check which ones are reasonable.

Write a new estimate for any that are unreasonable.

a) 151 – 29 is about 120

b) 94 – 37 is less than 40

c) 194 – 36 – 19 is about 130

d) 125 – 77 is close to 50

e) 72 – 33 is less than 20

f) 95 – 59 is close to 10

4 Round to the nearest 10 to estimate the answers to these number problems.

Number problem	Rounded estimation	Actual answer
22 + 37	20 + 40 = 60	59
37 + 92		
57 + 72		
88 – 33		
97 – 46		

⭐ **Challenge**

The children are selling raffle tickets. Nuria sells 98 tickets and Finlay sells 51 tickets. Finlay rounds both numbers to the nearest 100 and tells their teacher that they sold about the same number of tickets. Is this reasonable? Explain your answer.

1 Write the number written in each place value house in numerals and in words.

a)

H	T	O
2	8	5

Numerals: _____

Words: _____

b)

H	T	O
4	8	5

Numerals: _____

Words: _____

c)

H	T	O
4	1	5

Numerals: _____

Words: _____

d)

H	T	O
4	5	0

Numerals: _____

Words: _____

e)

H	T	O
9	1	4

Numerals: _____

Words: _____

f)

H	T	O
8	4	9

Numerals: _____

Words: _____

2 Draw a line from each card to the correct answer. One has been done for you.

Six hundred and twenty-four	3 hundreds, 1 tens and 5 ones
Eight hundred and thirty-three	5 hundreds, 5 tens and 7 ones
Eight hundred and eighteen	2 hundreds, 2 tens and 2 ones
Five hundred and fifty-seven	8 hundreds, 3 tens and 3 ones
Three hundred and fifteen	8 hundreds, 1 ten and 8 ones
Two hundred and twenty-two	6 hundreds, 2 tens and 4 ones

3 Sort the numbers into the table. Write them in numerals under the correct heading. Cross them out as you go. One has been done for you.

One hundred and seventeen

Three hundred and four

Seven hundred and fourteen

Four hundred and forty

Nine hundred and sixty-eight

Five hundred and three

Seven hundred and twelve

Five hundred and sixty-nine

Six hundred and seven

Two hundred and twenty

Numbers with no tens	Numbers with one ten	Numbers with more than five tens	Numbers with no ones
	117		

This is a game for 2 or more players.

You will need a pack of playing cards. Aces are used as ones.

Set aside all the 10s, jacks, queens and kings.

Shuffle the remaining cards.

Deal 3 cards to each player.

Each player uses their cards to make the biggest three-digit number they can and says their number out loud in words (for example, three hundred and twenty-two).

The person with the biggest number wins that round.

Variation:

After dealing the cards, place the remaining cards face down in a pile.

Players can then choose whether they want to swap one of their cards for a different one from the pile before making their number.

2.2 Zero as a place holder

1 Write the number written in each place value house in numerals and in words.

a)

H	T	O
1	0	9

Numerals: _____

Words: _____

b)

H	T	O
1	9	0

Numerals: _____

Words: _____

c)

H	T	O
2	0	4

Numerals: _____

Words: _____

d)

H	T	O
2	4	0

Numerals: _____

Words: _____

e)

H	T	O
6	3	0

Numerals: _____

Words: _____

f)

H	T	O
6	0	3

Numerals: _____

Words: _____

g)

H	T	O
9	1	0

Numerals: _____

Words: _____

h)

H	T	O
9	0	1

Numerals: _____

Words: _____

2) Complete the table.

Number	Number in numerals	Position of place holder
Six hundred and forty	640	in the ones position
Eight hundred and two		
Three hundred and four		
Seven hundred and eighty		
One hundred and eight		
Nine hundred and seven		
Two hundred and fifty		
Five hundred		
Five hundred and one		

3 Use the digit cards to make as many three-digit numbers as you can. Circle the biggest and the smallest numbers you make.

a)

0 2 9

○○○
○○○
○○○

b)

6 0 1

○○○
○○○
○○○

★ **Challenge**

Use the cards to make the number described.

a) 3 6 4   Make a three-digit number between 630 and 640.   ▢▢▢

b) 0 9 9   Make a three-digit number between 900 and 920.   ▢▢▢

c) 5 8 0   Make a three-digit number between 600 and 840.   ▢▢▢

13

2.3 Number sequences (1)

1 Write the numbers that are 10 more than:

a) 403 ☐   b) 430 ☐   c) 490 ☐

d) 329 ☐   e) 392 ☐   f) 302 ☐

2 Write the numbers that are 100 more than:

a) 624 ☐   b) 284 ☐   c) 894 ☐

d) 792 ☐   e) 92 ☐   f) 82 ☐

3 Write the numbers that are 10 less than:

a) 358 ☐   b) 385 ☐   c) 206 ☐

d) 506 ☐   e) 111 ☐   f) 101 ☐

4 Write the numbers that are 100 less than:

a) 112 ☐   b) 509 ☐   c) 299 ☐

d) 939 ☐   e) 303 ☐   f) 1000 ☐

5 Complete these number sequences.

a) 111, 211, ☐ , ☐ , ☐ , ☐ , ☐

b) 369, 379, ☐ , ☐ , ☐ , ☐ , ☐

c) 215, 205, ☐ , ☐ , ☐ , ☐ , ☐

d) 989, 889, ☐ , ☐ , ☐ , ☐ , ☐

6 Finlay has cut up a 1000 square. Fill in the empty boxes.

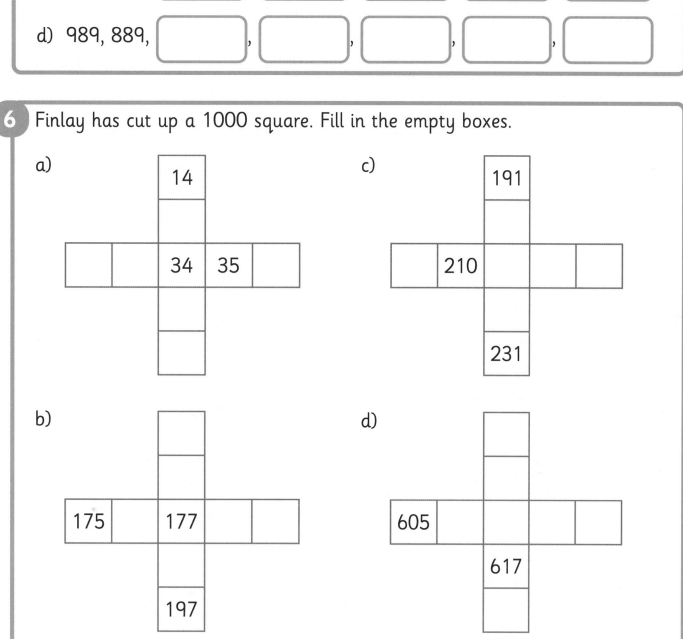

a)

```
        14
    34  35
```

c)

```
        191
  210
        231
```

b)

```
        
175   177
        197
```

d)

```
        
605
        617
```

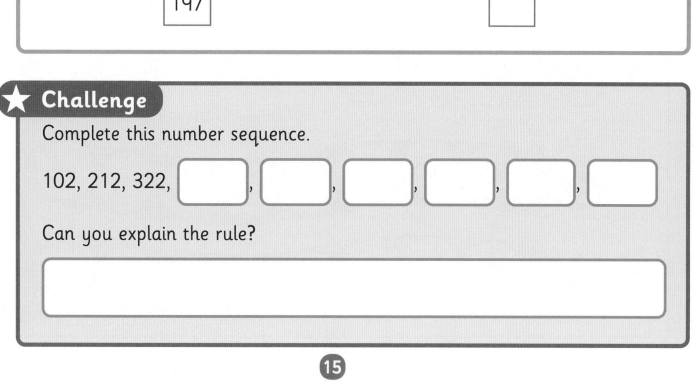

★ **Challenge**

Complete this number sequence.

102, 212, 322, ☐ , ☐ , ☐ , ☐ , ☐ , ☐

Can you explain the rule?

☐

2.4 Number sequences (2)

1 What are the missing numbers? Write them in.

a) (20) (40) ( ) (80)   b) (240) ( ) (280) (300)

c) (150) ( ) (250) (300)   d) (400) ( ) (500) ( )

e) (350) (375) ( ) (425)   f) (150) ( ) (200) (225)

2 Fill in the missing numbers by skip counting across the stones.

a) 240 260 ( ) ( ) 320 ( ) ( ) ( )

b) 740 760 ( ) ( ) ( ) 840 ( ) ( )

c)  150 200 ( ) ( ) ( ) 400 ( )

d) 600 650 ( ) ( ) ( ) ( ) ( )

e) 75 100 ( ) ( ) 175 ( ) ( ) ( )

f) 250 275 ( ) ( ) ( ) ( ) ( )

3 Choose your own starting number.

a) Skip count in 20s.

b) Skip count in 50s.

c) Skip count in 25s.

4 Work with a partner. Practise skip counting in 20s, 25s and 50s. Take it in turns to say the next number.

★ **Challenge**

Nuria is skip counting in 25s. If she starts at 300, how many skips will she take to get to 600?

How many skips if she starts at 175?

2.5 Number sequences (3)

1 Complete the number ladders.

a)		b)		c)		d)		e)	
280		920		560		550		890	
260		900		540		530		870	

What do you notice about the first and last numbers on each ladder?

2 Complete each number sequence.

a) | | | | | | | 650 | 700 |

b) | | | | | | | 675 | 700 |

c) | | | | | | | 680 | 700 |

d) | | | | | | 950 | 970 | |

e) | | | | 225 | 275 | | |

3

a) Skip count backwards in jumps of 50 to find the missing number.

| [ ] | | | | | | | 900 |

b) Skip count backwards in jumps of 25 to find the missing number.

| [ ] | | | | | | | 900 |

c) Skip count backwards in jumps of 20 to find the missing number.

| [ ] | | | | | | | 900 |

d) Skip count backwards in jumps of 25 to find the missing number.

| [ ] | | | | | | | 450 |

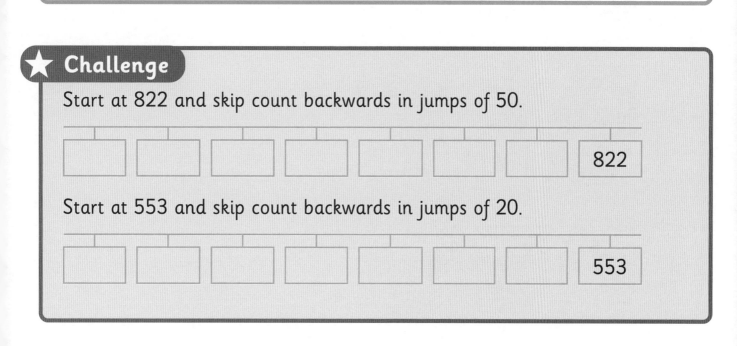

★ **Challenge**

Start at 822 and skip count backwards in jumps of 50.

| [ ] | [ ] | [ ] | [ ] | [ ] | [ ] | [ ] | 822 |

Start at 553 and skip count backwards in jumps of 20.

| [ ] | [ ] | [ ] | [ ] | [ ] | [ ] | [ ] | 553 |

1 Write each number shown in numerals and in words.

a)

Numerals: _____

Words: _____

b)

Numerals: _____

Words: _____

c)

Numerals: _____

Words: _____

d)

Numerals: _____

Words: _____

e)

Numerals: _____

Words: _____

f)

Numerals: _____

Words: _____

2 In the number 342, the value of the 4 is four tens or 40. The value of the 3 is three hundreds or 300. The value of the 2 is two ones or 2.

Write the value of the underlined digit in these numbers, in both words and numerals.

a) 5<u>4</u>1

b) <u>9</u>03

c) 4<u>8</u>8

d) 40<u>2</u>

e) 5<u>6</u>9

3 Draw a representation of each number. You could use base 10 blocks to help you, or dot squares and strips. Check your drawing by asking a friend to say what number it is.

a) 199

b) 309

c) 352

d) 720

a) Write a three-digit number with a tens digit value of more than 40 and a hundreds digit value of less than 300.

b) Write a three-digit number with a hundreds digit value between 300 and 600, a tens digit value of more than 60 and a ones digit value of 7.

2.7 Standard place value partitioning of three-digit numbers

1 Write down each number shown by the arrow cards.

a) `4 0 0` `6 0` `1` = ____

b) `7 0 0` `6 0` `8` = ____

c) `1 0 0` `2 0` `5` = ____

d) `9 0 0` `1 0` `4` = ____

e) `8 0 0` `8 0` `7` = ____

f) `3 0 0` `5 0` `1` = ____

2 Fill in the arrow cards to make each number.

a) 395 =

b) 222 =

c) 853 =

d) 136 =

e) 491 =

f) 918 =

3 Write the number represented by each set of base 10 blocks, then partition it into hundreds, tens and ones. One has been done for you.

a)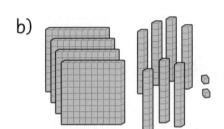

Numerals: _____272_____

Partition: _____200 + 70 + 2_____

b)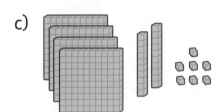

Numerals: _____

Partition: _____

c)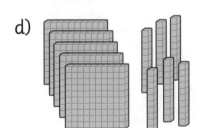

Numerals: _____

Partition: _____

d)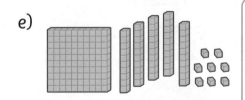

Numerals: _____

Partition: _____

e)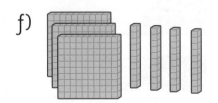

Numerals: _____

Partition: _____

f)

Numerals: _____

Partition: _____

4 Complete the totals. One has been done for you.

a)

100 100 100 10 10 1
100 100 10 10

[5] hundreds, [4] tens and [1] one = [500] + [40] + [1] = [541]

b)

100 100 100 10 10 1 1 1
100 100 100

[ ] hundreds, [ ] tens and [ ] one = [ ] + [ ] + [ ] = [ ]

c)

100 100 100 100 100 10 10 1 1
100 100 100 100 10 1

[ ] hundreds, [ ] tens and [ ] one = [ ] + [ ] + [ ] = [ ]

d)

100 100 100 10 10 10 10

[ ] hundreds, [ ] tens and [ ] one = [ ] + [ ] + [ ] = [ ]

e)

100 10 10 10 10 1 1 1 1

[ ] hundreds, [ ] tens and [ ] one = [ ] + [ ] + [ ] = [ ]

f)

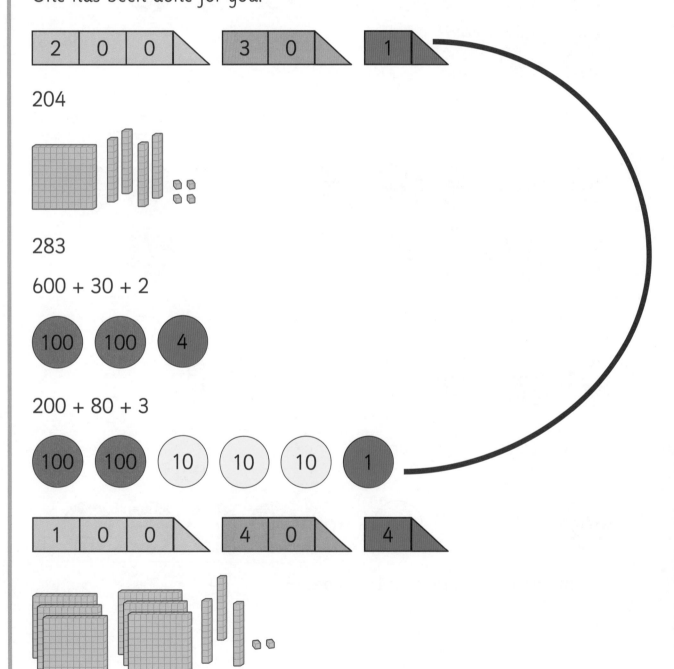

(100) (100) (100) (100) (1) (1) (1)

(100) (100) (100) (100) (1) (1) (1)

⬚ hundreds, ⬚ tens and ⬚ one = ⬚ + ⬚ + ⬚ = ⬚

---

5 Draw lines to connect the representations that show the same number. One has been done for you.

| 2 | 0 | 0 | ◣ | 3 | 0 | ◣ | 1 | ◣

204

283

600 + 30 + 2

(100) (100) (4)

200 + 80 + 3

(100) (100) (10) (10) (10) (1)

| 1 | 0 | 0 | ◣ | 4 | 0 | ◣ | 4 | ◣

6 These numbers have been partitioned into hundreds, tens and ones.

Write the numbers.

a) 300   50   4   [   ]

b) 4   50   200   [   ]

c) 40   500   2   [   ]

d) 600   3   80   [   ]

e) 100   20   1   [   ]

f) 8   500   70   [   ]

g) 90   1   600   [   ]

★ Challenge

a) Nuria is thinking of a three-digit number. Two of the digits are the same and the third digit is zero. The sum of all three digits is 10.

What is Nuria's number? Make a list of all the possibilities.

[   ]

b) Finlay is thinking of a different three-digit number. The hundreds digit is an odd number with a value greater than 500. The sum of the other two digits is 4. None of the digits are the same.

What is Finlay's number? Make a list of all the possibilities.

[   ]

2.8 Non-standard place value partitioning of two-digit numbers

1 Partition each number in 4 different ways.

You can use base ten blocks or place value counters.

a) 47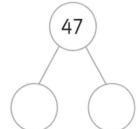

b) 95

c) 78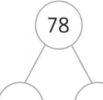

d) 64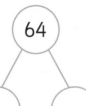

e) 51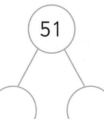

2 Find the missing number to complete each partition.

a)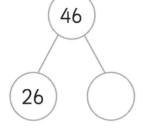

b)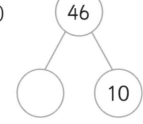

c)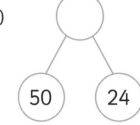

d)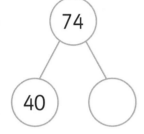

e)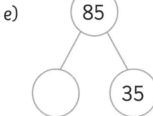

f)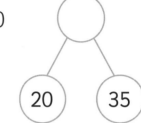

3 Partition each of these numbers using standard place value partitioning and then write down a non-standard partition. One has been done for you.

Number	Standard partition	Non-standard partition
99	90 + 9	50 + 49
66		
48		
35		
28		

★ **Challenge**

Amman says that 300 + 20 + 40 + 10 + 2 is a non-standard partition of the number 372. Is he right?

Explain your answer.

1 For each pair of numbers, write < or > to make the number statement true.

a) 50 [ ] 500

b) 50 [ ] 35

c) 375 [ ] 378

d) 887 [ ] 878

e) 919 [ ] 929

f) 744 [ ] 774

2 For each statement, tick TRUE or FALSE. If the statement is false, change the symbol =, >, <, or ≠ to make it true.

a) 67 = 670   TRUE   FALSE   [ ]

b) 67 > 670   TRUE   FALSE   [ ]

c) 530 > 53   TRUE   FALSE   [ ]

d) 42 ≠ 402   TRUE   FALSE   [ ]

e) 199 > 200   TRUE   FALSE   [ ]

f) 153 > 135   TRUE   FALSE   [ ]

g) 420 < 402   TRUE   FALSE   [ ]

3 Rearrange each set of digit cards to make a number that makes the statement true.

The first one has been done for you.

a) ⬜3⬜ ⬜4⬜ ⬜7⬜ 〈<〉 ⬜4⬜ ⬜7⬜ ⬜3⬜

b) ⬜2⬜ ⬜3⬜ ⬜1⬜ 〈>〉 ⬜ ⬜ ⬜

c) ⬜3⬜ ⬜5⬜ ⬜0⬜ 〈<〉 ⬜ ⬜ ⬜

d) ⬜7⬜ ⬜0⬜ ⬜7⬜ 〈<〉 ⬜ ⬜ ⬜

e) ⬜6⬜ ⬜3⬜ ⬜0⬜ 〈>〉 ⬜ ⬜ ⬜

f) ⬜4⬜ ⬜9⬜ ⬜2⬜ 〈>〉 ⬜ ⬜ ⬜

g) ⬜1⬜ ⬜1⬜ ⬜3⬜ 〈<〉 ⬜ ⬜ ⬜

h) What symbol could you use instead of < and > which would make the statements true?

⬜⬜⬜⬜⬜⬜⬜⬜⬜⬜⬜⬜⬜⬜⬜⬜

★ **Challenge**

⬜ ⬜3⬜ ⬜ ◯ ⬜ ⬜ ⬜3⬜

Use one of the symbols and every digit to make **true** number statements. How many can you make?

< > 5 2 2 1

2.10 Ordering two- and three-digit numbers

1 Write each set of numbers in order, from smallest to largest.

a) 522, 376, 48, 988, 108

b) 152, 135, 125, 140, 134

c) 616, 630, 306, 613, 361

d) 934, 900, 917, 943, 925

2 Write each set of numbers in order, from largest to smallest.

a) 403, 340, 304, 433, 430

b) 791, 179, 968, 869, 798

c) 212, 22, 202, 222, 220

d) 394, 499, 383, 399, 483

3 Write each set of numbers under the correct arrows on the number lines.

a) 148, 65, 117, 101, 124

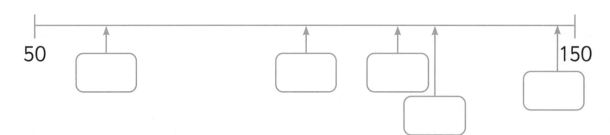

50   150

b) 554, 601, 595, 503, 539

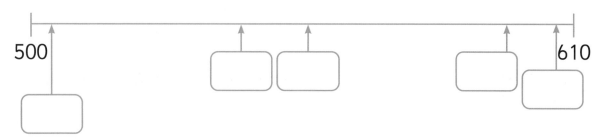

500   610

c) 288, 321, 260, 233, 271

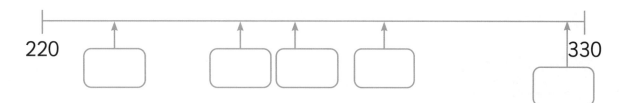

220   330

d) 396, 963, 693, 639, 336

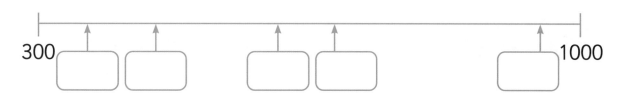

300   1000

★ Challenge

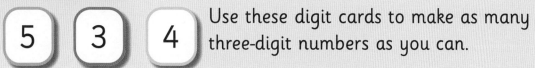

5   **3**   **4**   Use these digit cards to make as many three-digit numbers as you can.

Use each digit only once in each number.

Write them down, then put them in order on the empty number line below.

You will need to think about where the number line starts and finishes.

2.11 Ordinal Numbers

1 Draw lines to match the pairs of ordinal numbers.

412th	four hundred and twenty-eighth
32nd	thirty-second
428th	five hundred and first
323rd	four hundred and twelfth
501st	five hundred and eightieth
580th	three hundred and twenty-third

2 Write the ordinal numbers in words.

a) 250th

b) 92nd

c) 311th

d) 601st

e) 43rd

3

Amman's dad

A · B

Amman's dad is running a marathon. There are many runners in front of him and many behind him.

Out of all the runners, he is 342nd.

Write down the position of each of the women dressed in blue (A and B), in words and numerals.

Woman A:

Woman B:

★ Challenge

Nuria is building a staircase out of blocks. This diagram shows the first, second and third steps. How many blocks will she need to build the 30th step? What about the 122nd step?

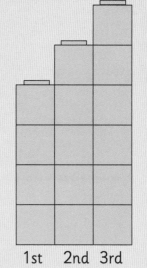

1st   2nd   3rd

3.1 Adding and subtracting a one-digit number to and from a three-digit number

1 Finlay is adding and subtracting one digit numbers to and from three-digit numbers. He decides to partition the one-digit number to find the nearest 10.

For each question, tick the partition Finlay should use.

a) 126 + 8

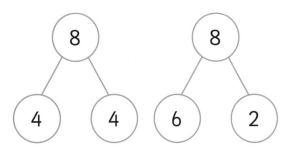

b) 374 + 9

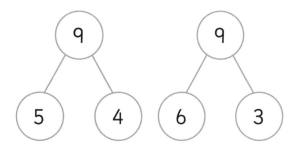

c) 297 + 7

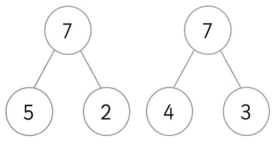

d) 533 + 8

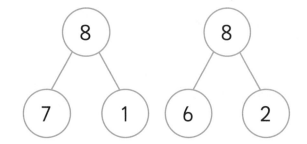

e) 745 – 9

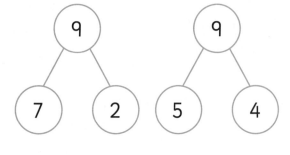

f) 834 – 7

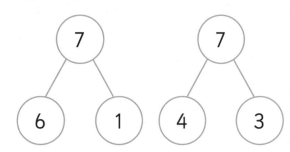

2 Use your known facts and place value to help you answer each set of questions.

a) 5 + 4 = ☐

   125 + 4 = ☐

   145 + 4 = ☐

b) 6 + 6 = ☐

   106 + 6 = ☐

   136 + 6 = ☐

c) 9 − 6 = ☐

   119 − 6 = ☐

   149 − 6 = ☐

d) 13 − 8 = ☐

   213 − 8 = ☐

   613 − 8 = ☐

3 Complete these number sentences.

a) 364 + 8 = ☐

b) 365 + 7 = ☐

c) 385 + 8 = ☐

d) 249 + 9 = ☐

e) 723 − 2 = ☐

f) 733 − 4 = ☐

★ **Challenge**

Nuria is adding one-digit numbers to three-digit numbers. She adds 6 using this partition.

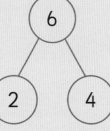

Write down 3 different three-digit numbers that she could use this partition to add 6 to.

☐

What do you notice?

☐

3.2 Adding and subtracting 10 and 100

1 Add 10 to each number. Write your answers in the place value houses.

a)

H	T	O
3	6	9

Add 10 ➡

H	T	O

b)

H	T	O
4	6	9

Add 10 ➡

H	T	O

c)

H	T	O
4	7	9

Add 10 ➡

H	T	O

d)

H	T	O
5	9	9

Add 10 ➡

H	T	O

e)

H	T	O
6	9	3

Add 10 ➡

H	T	O

f)

H	T	O
8	7	3

Add 10 ➡

H	T	O

2 Subtract 10 from each number. Write your answers in the place value houses.

a)

H	T	O
7	4	2

Subtract 10 →

H	T	O

b)

H	T	O
7	7	2

Subtract 10 →

H	T	O

c)

H	T	O
7	1	2

Subtract 10 →

H	T	O

d)

H	T	O
7	0	2

Subtract 10 →

H	T	O

e)

H	T	O
4	0	2

Subtract 10 →

H	T	O

f)

H	T	O
4	0	8

Subtract 10 →

H	T	O

3 Complete these addition problems.

a) 127 + 100 = ☐   b) 527 + 100 = ☐

c) 507 + 100 = ☐   d) 503 + 100 = ☐

e) 703 + 100 = ☐   f) 723 + 100 = ☐

4 Complete these subtraction problems.

a) 911 – 100 = ☐   b) 611 – 100 = ☐

c) 691 – 100 = ☐   d) 698 – 100 = ☐

e) 498 – 100 = ☐   f) 408 – 100 = ☐

5 Complete these number sentences.

a) 858 – 10 = ☐   b) ☐ + 100 = 459

c) 632 + ☐ = 642   d) 381 – 100 = ☐

e) ☐ – 10 = 892   f) 117 + ☐ = 127

g) 591 + 10 = ☐   h) ☐ + 100 = 718

★ Challenge

Now try these:

a) 683 + 10 – 100 = ☐   b) 409 – 10 + 100 = ☐

c) 316 + 10 + 10 + 100 = ☐   d) ☐ + 100 – 10 = 127

e) 482 – 100 – 10 – 10 = ☐   f) ☐ – 10 – 100 = 699

3.3 Adding and subtracting multiples of 10 and 100

1 Work out how many hundreds there are in each number then solve the problem. One has been done for you.

a) 200 + 600 = [2 hundreds + 6 hundreds = 8 hundreds = 800]

b) 900 – 300 = [   ]

c) 400 + 500 = [   ]

d) 700 – 200 = [   ]

2 Add or subtract the multiples of 100.

a) 500 + 300 = [   ]   b) 565 + 300 = [   ]

c) 265 + 300 = [   ]   d) 269 + 500 = [   ]

e) 800 – 200 = [   ]   f) 842 – 200 = [   ]

g) 642 – 200 = [   ]   h) 681 – 400 = [   ]

3 Finlay uses place value to calculate 631 + 40.

He knows that 631 = 600 + 30 + 1, so 631 + 40 = 600 + 30 + 40 + 1 = 671

Use Finlay's method to solve these addition and subtraction problems.

a) 631 + 60 = [   ] + [   ] + [   ] + [   ] = [   ]

b) 185 – 60 = [   ] + [   ] – [   ] + [   ] = [   ]

c) 826 + 70 = [   ] + [   ] + [   ] + [   ] = [   ]

d) 672 − 40 = [   ] + [   ] − [   ] + [   ] = [   ]

e) 617 + 50 = [   ] + [   ] − [   ] + [   ] = [   ]

f) 299 − 70 = [   ] + [   ] + [   ] + [   ] = [   ]

4 Write a number sentence for each number line. One has been done for you.

a)

572   592   602   612

612 − 40 = 572

b) 452   532

[   ]

c) 169   229

[   ]

d) 763   833

[   ]

e) 165   255

[   ]

5 Draw your own empty number lines to show how to solve these problems.

a) 391 + 30

391

b) 532 – 50

532

c) 582 + 60

582

d) 616 – 40

616

Amman has made up a rule to make a number sequence. The rule is to add 10, then 20, then 30 and so on.

Amman starts at 243. Write down the first 6 numbers in his sequence.

Next, he starts at 101. This makes a sequence that starts 101, 111, 131, ...

What will Amman's 6th number be?

What will his 10th number be?

1 Use the empty number line to help you complete the number sentences.
One has been done for you.

a) $46 + \boxed{54} = 100$

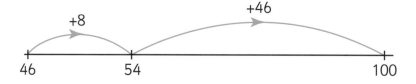

b) $77 + \boxed{} = 100$

c) $25 + \boxed{} = 100$

d) $21 + \boxed{} = 100$

e) $100 - 48 = \boxed{}$

f) $100 - 54 = \boxed{}$

g) $100 - 16 = \boxed{}$

2 Complete the bar models, then write the fact family. One has been done for you.

a)

100			
33	67		

$33 + 67 = 100$	$100 - 33 = 67$
$67 + 33 = 100$	$100 - 67 = 33$

b)

100
53	

c)

d)

3 Use partitioning to check if each number sentence is true or false. Tick the true number sentences. Change one digit in each false number sentence to make it true.

a) 36 + 74 = 100 ☐

b) 54 + 46 = 100 ☐

c) 25 + 85 = 100 ☐

d) 19 + 91 = 100 ☐

e) 38 + 63 = 100 ☐

f) 73 + 27 = 100 ☐

★ **Challenge**

Solve these problems. Show how you worked each problem out.

a) Finlay has £1.00. He buys a packet of crisps for 58p. How much change does he receive?

b) Isla wants to buy a pencil that costs £1.00, but she only has 83p. How much more money does she need?

c) 100 children and their teachers are going on a school trip. One bus can carry 42 people. How many buses will they need?

3.5 Doubling and halving

1 Draw lines to connect the right answer to each calculation.

| 40 + 40 | 70 + 70 | 120 – 60 | 180 – 90 | 600 – 300 | 400 + 400 |

| 800 | 140 | 60 | 80 | 90 | 300 |

2 Double each number using partitioning. One has been done for you.

a) 68 [60] + [60] and [8] + [8] ➡ [120] + [16] = [136]

b) 35 [ ] + [ ] and [ ] + [ ] ➡ [ ] + [ ] = [ ]

c) 53 [ ] + [ ] and [ ] + [ ] ➡ [ ] + [ ] = [ ]

d) 44 [ ] + [ ] and [ ] + [ ] ➡ [ ] + [ ] = [ ]

e) 29 [ ] + [ ] and [ ] + [ ] ➡ [ ] + [ ] = [ ]

f) 86 [ ] + [ ] and [ ] + [ ] ➡ [ ] + [ ] = [ ]

3 Halve each number using partitioning. One has been done for you.

a) 38 Half of [30] is [15] and half of [8] is [4] ➡ [15] + [4] = [19]

b) 82 Half of [ ] is [ ] and half of [ ] is [ ] ➡ [ ] + [ ] = [ ]

c) 66 Half of [ ] is [ ] and half of [ ] is [ ] ➡ [ ] + [ ] = [ ]

d) 54 Half of [ ] is [ ] and half of [ ] is [ ] ➡ [ ] + [ ] = [ ]

e) 72 Half of [ ] is [ ] and half of [ ] is [ ] ➡ [ ] + [ ] = [ ]

f) 110 Half of [ ] is [ ] and half of [ ] is [ ] ➡ [ ] + [ ] = [ ]

4 Now try these.

a) Double 39 is [ ]

b) Double 69 is [ ]

c) Half of 56 is [ ]

d) Half of 106 is [ ]

e) Double 18 is [ ]

f) Double 48 is [ ]

g) Half of 48 is [ ]

h) Half of 78 is [ ]

★ **Challenge**

Isla thinks of a number. She doubles it, doubles it again, then doubles it a third time and gets the number 56. What number was Isla thinking of?

[ ]

Amman starts with a two-digit number. He halves it, then halves it again, then halves it a third time and gets the number 12. What number did he start with?

[ ]

3.6 Adding a string of numbers

1 Draw lines to connect the numbers which total a multiple of 10.

23

35

11

65

84

42

38

17

69

56

2 Add the numbers which total a multiple of 10 first. Then add the remaining number. The first one has been done for you.

a) 12 + 15 + 38 = | 50 | + | 15 | = | 65 |

b) 25 + 26 + 34 = [ ] + [ ] = [ ]

c) 18 + 52 + 13 = [ ] + [ ] = [ ]

d) 39 + 22 + 21 = [ ] + [ ] = [ ]

e) 45 + 35 + 12 = [ ] + [ ] = [ ]

f) 16 + 43 + 24 = [ ] + [ ] = [ ]

g) 18 + 18 + 32 = [ ] + [ ] = [ ]

3 Add these number strings by finding pairs of numbers which add to make a multiple of 10. Make jottings to help you solve them.

a) (3) (15) (25) (17) (11) ( )

b) (8) (14) (35) (22) (6) ( )

c) (17) (48) (21) (9) (2) ( )

d) (51) (15) (9) (5) (40) ( )

e) (28) (13) (7) (25) (12) ( )

f) (8) (7) (22) (66) (3) ( )

★ **Challenge**

Write down any 4 different two-digit numbers which are not multiples of 10, but when added together, make a multiple of 10.

[ ] + [ ] + [ ] + [ ] = [ ]

Is it possible to add 5 different two-digit numbers, which are not multiples of 10, to give a total which is a multiple of 10? Show your thinking.

1 Find the answers to these questions using round and adjust.

Use the number lines to show your working.

a) 44 + 9

44 + 10 = 54   So 44 + 9 = 53

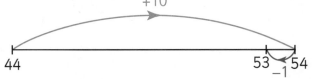

+10

44   53   54
                        −1

b) 84 + 9

84 + 10 = ☐   so 84 + 9 = ☐

c) 51 − 9

51 − 10 = ☐   so 51 − 9 = ☐

d) 91 − 9

91 − 10 = ☐   so 91 − 9 = ☐

e) 76 − 9

76 − 10 = ☐   so 76 − 9 = ☐

f) 45 + 9

45 + 10 = ☐   so 45 + 9 = ☐

2 Find the answers to these questions.

Use the number lines to show your working.

a) 73 + 8

$|$ ———————————————————————— $|$

73 + 10 = [ ]   so 73 + 8 = [ ]

b) 33 + 8

$|$ ———————————————————————— $|$

33 + 10 = [ ]   so 33 + 8 = [ ]

c) 73 – 8

$|$ ———————————————————————— $|$

73 – 10 = [ ]   so 73 – 8 = [ ]

3 Complete each number sentence. Explain to a partner how you solved it.

a) 62 + [ ] = 70

b) [ ] + 8 = 83

c) 55 + [ ] = 63

d) [ ] + 9 = 26

★ **Challenge**

Amman writes a number sequence. He starts at 93 then subtracts 9 each time. Write down the first 8 numbers of Amman's number sequence. What do you notice?

[ ]

What happens if he starts at 80? What do you notice?

[ ]

1 Make a bar model for each subtraction. Then use a strategy of your choice to find the answer. Use the same numbers to write an addition partner for each subtraction.

a) 71 − 40 = ☐　☐ + ☐ = ☐

b) 88 − 44 = ☐　☐ + ☐ = ☐

c) 58 − 16 = ☐　☐ + ☐ = ☐

d) 90 − 9 = ☐　☐ + ☐ = ☐

e) 66 − 25 = ☐　☐ + ☐ = ☐

f) 73 − 66 = ☐　☐ + ☐ = ☐

2 Choose strategy **A** or strategy **B** to solve each problem. Show your working.

A Add or subtract 10 then adjust

B Count on or count back on a number line

Circle the strategy you used.

a) 125 + 9 = ☐　A　B

b) 302 − 4 = ☐　A　B

c) 156 − 8 = ☐　A　B

d) 795 + 7 = ☐　A　B

e) 450 − 11 = ☐　A　B

3 Solve these number problems. Explain to a partner how you worked each answer out.

a) $852 + \boxed{} = 861$

b) $\boxed{} + 210 = 420$

c) $308 + 8 = \boxed{}$

d) $\boxed{} - 8 = 309$

e) $650 - \boxed{} = 325$

f) $\boxed{} - 6 = 300$

g) $145 = 154 - \boxed{}$

h) $12 + 7 + 28 + 5 = \boxed{}$

★ **Challenge**

Amman's favourite strategy is using known number facts. He tries to use this strategy to solve $402 - 8$. Is this a useful strategy?

What would be a better strategy to use? Solve the problem and draw a representation of how you solved it.

3.9 Solving word problems

For each problem, complete a bar model to help you work out whether the whole or one of the parts is unknown.

Write a number sentence to match your bar model then solve the problem using a strategy of your choice.

1 Isla is baking a cake. She needs 275 grams of flour. She puts some flour onto her weighing scale and it says 225 grams. How much more flour does Isla need?

275

225	?

$225 + ? = 275$

Isla needs ⬚ more grams of flour.

2 Finlay's mum spent twice as much money on groceries this week than last week. If she spent £84 this week, how much did she spend last week?

Finlay's mum spent ⬚ on groceries last week.

3 245 people board an aeroplane and sit down. There are 9 empty seats left. How many seats does the aeroplane have?

The aeroplane has ⬚ seats.

4 There are 89 adults and some children at a wedding. There are 115 people altogether. How many children are there?

There are ⬚ children at the wedding.

5 On a pond, there are half as many swans as there are ducks. There are 78 ducks. How many swans are there?

There are ⬚ swans.

6 Finlay is planting seeds. He plants 305 seeds. A bird eats 8 of them. How many seeds are there now?

There are ⬚ seeds.

7 There are 172 children in a playground. 12 more arrive. How many children are in the playground now?

There are ☐ children in the playground now.

8 Amman has 107 apples. He puts 19 of them into a blue box and the rest into a red box. How many apples are in the red box?

There are ☐ apples in the red box.

9 A man has two fifty-pound notes. He buys a jacket that costs £68. How much change will he get from his two fifty-pound notes?

He will get £ ☐ change.

Nuria wants to buy 100 cupcakes for her party. The table shows how many cupcakes she buys from each stall.

Stall Number	Number of cupcakes bought
1	33
2	6
3	14
4	23

How many cupcakes has Nuria bought? Write a number sentence to show how you worked it out.

Stall 5 has 22 cupcakes for sale. If Nuria buys them all, will she have enough for her party? Explain your thinking.

1 Keep the larger number whole and partition the smaller number.

Draw an empty number line for each addition, then solve it.

Compare number lines and answers with a partner.

a) 843 + 57 = 843 + 50 + 7   843 + 57 = ☐

```
+————————————————————+
843
```

b) 743 + 88 = 743 + ☐   743 + 88 = ☐

```
+————————————————————+
743
```

c) 29 + 643 = ☐   29 + 643 = ☐

```
+————————————————————+
```

d) 48 + 672 = ☐   48 + 672 = ☐

```
+————————————————————+
```

e) 272 + 28 = ☐   272 + 28 = ☐

```
+————————————————————+
```

f) 572 + 69 = ☐   572 + 69 = ☐

```
+————————————————————+
```

2 Write down 2 different strategies you could use to solve 458 + 29

3 Solve these addition problems. Use the strategy you feel most confident with.

a) 56 + 219 = ⬚

b) 606 + 19 = ⬚

c) 33 + 447 = ⬚

d) 447 + 55 = ⬚

e) 620 + 91 = ⬚

f) 618 + 92 = ⬚

g) 312 + 58 = ⬚

h) 58 + 809 = ⬚

 Challenge

Use every digit card to complete the calculation.

| 3 | 4 | 5 | 6 | 7 |

⬚ ⬚ ⬚ + ⬚ ⬚ = 439

Compare with a friend. Did you make the same calculation?

1 Use an empty number line to help you calculate:

a) 628 – 59 = [ ]

⊢———————————————————————————⊣
628

b) 328 – 69 = [ ]

⊢———————————————————————————⊣
328

c) 528 – 66 = [ ]

⊢———————————————————————————⊣
528

d) 343 – 56 = [ ]

⊢———————————————————————————⊣

e) 123 – 46 = [ ]

⊢———————————————————————————⊣

f) 243 – 84 = [ ]

⊢———————————————————————————⊣

g) 245 – 83 = [ ]

⊢———————————————————————————⊣

2 Use partitioning to help you solve these calculations. You may choose to use place value counters. The first one has been done for you.

a) 848 − 32

848 = [800] + [40] + [8], and 32 = [30] + [2]

[40] − [30] = [10], and [8] − [2] = [6]

so 848 − 32 = [800] + [10] + [6] = [816]

b) 888 − 42

888 = [　　] + [　　] + [　　], and 42 = [　　] + [　　]

[　　] − [　　] = [　　], and [　　] − [　　] = [　　]

so 888 − 42 = [　　] + [　　] + [　　] = [　　]

c) 448 − 46

448 = [　　] + [　　] + [　　], and 46 = [　　] + [　　]

[　　] − [　　] = [　　], and [　　] − [　　] = [　　]

so 448 − 46 = [　　] + [　　] + [　　] = [　　]

d) 459 − 56

459 = [　　] + [　　] + [　　], and 56 = [　　] + [　　]

[　　] − [　　] = [　　], and [　　] − [　　] = [　　]

so 459 − 56 = [　　] + [　　] + [　　] = [　　]

e) 599 − 23

599 = [ ] + [ ] + [ ], and 23 = [ ] + [ ]

[ ] − [ ] = [ ], and [ ] − [ ] = [ ]

so 599 − 23 = [ ] + [ ] + [ ] = [ ]

f) 577 − 23

577 = [ ] + [ ] + [ ], and 23 = [ ] + [ ]

[ ] − [ ] = [ ], and [ ] − [ ] = [ ]

so 577 − 23 = [ ] + [ ] + [ ] = [ ]

3 Solve these calculations using whichever strategy you feel most confident with. Use jottings to help you. Talk to a partner about the strategies you used.

a) 186 − 95 = [ ]

b) 417 − 52 = [ ]

c) 399 − 64 = [ ]

d) 402 − 64 = [ ]

e) 981 − 29 = [ ]

f) 448 − 39 = [ ]

g) 273 − 54 = [ ]

4 Now try these.

a) 615 – 82 ☐

b) 625 – 82 ☐

c) 625 – 92 ☐

d) 605 – 92 ☐

What do you notice?

☐

Nuria and Finlay are solving the problem 305 – ? = 27.

Finlay says he will use partitioning to solve the problem. Nuria wants to use a number line.

Whose strategy do you prefer, and why?

☐

Solve 305 - ? = 27. ☐

What strategy did you use to solve it?

☐

3.12 Adding three-digit numbers

1 Use the number line to calculate the answers to these additions.

a)   384
   + 197
   ⎯⎯⎯⎯⎯

   ⎯⎯⎯⎯⎯

b)   384
   + 248
   ⎯⎯⎯⎯⎯

   ⎯⎯⎯⎯⎯

c)   384
   + 542
   ⎯⎯⎯⎯⎯

   ⎯⎯⎯⎯⎯

d)   736
   + 185
   ⎯⎯⎯⎯⎯

   ⎯⎯⎯⎯⎯

e)   391
   + 185
   ⎯⎯⎯⎯⎯

   ⎯⎯⎯⎯⎯

f)   391
   + 274
   ⎯⎯⎯⎯⎯

   ⎯⎯⎯⎯⎯

g)   511
   + 274
   ⎯⎯⎯⎯⎯

2 Solve the additions by partitioning the numbers. One has been done for you.

a)
```
   277
 + 412
   689
```
200 and 70 and 7
400 and 10 and 2
600 and 80 and 9 = 689

b)
```
   415
 + 277
```
_____

_____

c)
```
   279
 + 301
```
_____

_____

d)
```
   551
 + 363
```
_____

_____

e)
```
   551
 + 284
```
_____

_____

f)
```
   442
 + 374
```
_____

_____

g)
```
   374
 + 508
```
_____

_____

3 Finlay needs to work out 246 + 199. He says, "I know that 199 is one less than 200. 246 + 200 is 446. But I have added one too many. I need to adjust my answer by taking one away. So 246 + 199 = 445."

Use Finlay's strategy to solve these problems.

a) 650 + 299 = ☐

b) 450 + 199 = ☐

c) 358 + 299 = ☐

d) 299 + 601 = ☐

4 Complete the number statements.

a) 255 + ☐ = 520

b) 143 + ☐ = 255

c) ☐ + 343 = 684

d) ☐ + 209 = 353

5 Add the numbers.

a) 199 + 451 + 249 = ☐

b) 308 + 140 + 260 = ☐

c) 101 + 258 + 399 = ☐

d) 230 + 230 + 212 = ☐

Which digits are hidden by the splats?

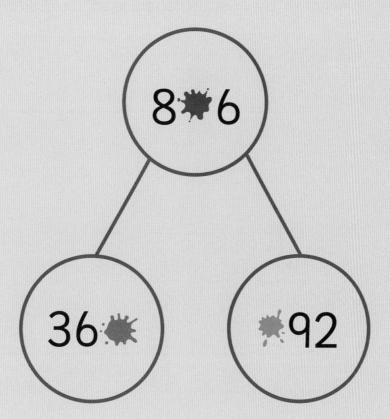

1 Calculate the answers to these subtraction problems using the empty number line.

a)
$$\begin{array}{r} 605 \\ -\ 396 \\ \hline \\ \hline \end{array}$$

605

b)
$$\begin{array}{r} 605 \\ -\ 217 \\ \hline \\ \hline \end{array}$$

605

c)
$$\begin{array}{r} 625 \\ -\ 427 \\ \hline \\ \hline \end{array}$$

625

d)
$$\begin{array}{r} 728 \\ -\ 427 \\ \hline \\ \hline \end{array}$$

e)
$$\begin{array}{r} 427 \\ -\ 308 \\ \hline \\ \hline \end{array}$$

f)
$$\begin{array}{r} 500 \\ -\ 314 \\ \hline \\ \hline \end{array}$$

g)
$$\begin{array}{r} 314 \\ -\ 266 \\ \hline \\ \hline \end{array}$$

2 Solve these subtraction problems using partitioning. One has been done for you.

a)
$$\begin{array}{r} 499 \\ -\ 165 \\ \hline 334 \\ \hline \end{array}$$

400 and 90 and 9
$-$ 100 and 60 and 5
_____
300 and 30 and 4 = 334

b)
$$\begin{array}{r} 499 \\ -\ 334 \\ \hline \\ \hline \end{array}$$
_____

c)
$$\begin{array}{r} 788 \\ -\ 535 \\ \hline \\ \hline \end{array}$$
_____

d)
$$\begin{array}{r} 878 \\ -\ 535 \\ \hline \\ \hline \end{array}$$
_____

e)
$$\begin{array}{r} 693 \\ -\ 353 \\ \hline \\ \hline \end{array}$$
_____

f)
$$\begin{array}{r} 693 \\ -\ 142 \\ \hline \\ \hline \end{array}$$
_____

3 Draw a line to match the missing number to each diagram.

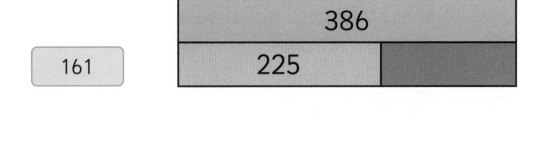

161

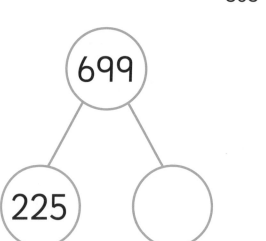

474

578

4 Complete the table. The first one has been done for you.

Bigger number	Smaller number	Difference
762	462	300
799	501	
	297	203
688		426

5 Decide if each number sentence is true or false and tick your answer. Change each false statement to make it **true**.

a) 378 − 99 = 368   **TRUE**   **FALSE**   [ ]

b) 456 − 199 = 257   **TRUE**   **FALSE**   [ ]

c) 566 − 299 = 267   **TRUE**   **FALSE**   [ ]

d) 751 − 299 = 450   **TRUE**   **FALSE**   [ ]

e) 645 − 399 = 244   **TRUE**   **FALSE**   [ ]

f) 450 − 98 = 352   **TRUE**   **FALSE**   [ ]

★ Challenge

Amman is checking his subtraction calculations by adding.

a) He subtracts 150 from 475 and gets 325. To check, he adds 325 + 150 and gets 475.

Was Amman's subtraction correct? Show your working.

[ ]

b) Amman subtracts two different numbers and checks his calculations by adding. One of the numbers in the calculation is 486 and another is 230.

What could his calculations have been? There are two possible answers.

[ ] + [ ] = 486 ➡ [ ] − [ ] = 230

[ ] + 486 = [ ] ➡ [ ] − [ ] = 230

3.14 Representing and solving word problems

Complete a Think Board for each question, then solve the problem.

1

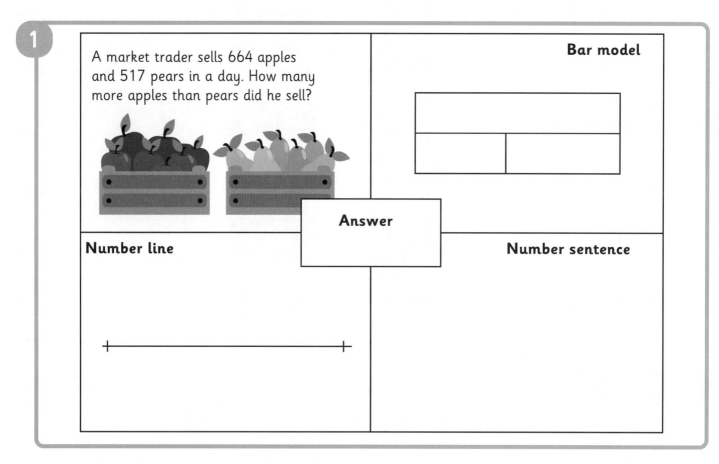

A market trader sells 664 apples and 517 pears in a day. How many more apples than pears did he sell?

Bar model

Answer

Number line

Number sentence

2

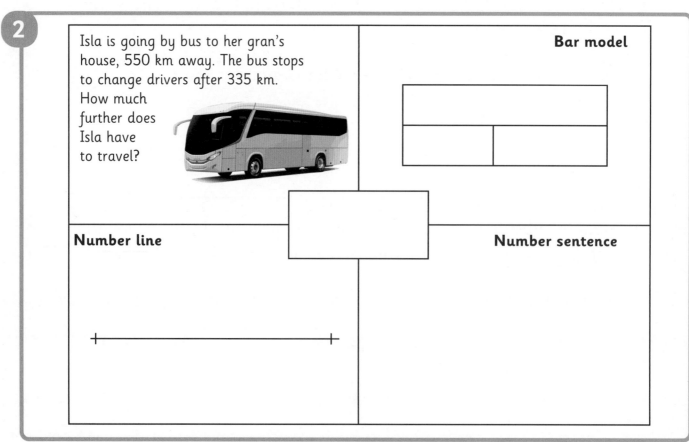

Isla is going by bus to her gran's house, 550 km away. The bus stops to change drivers after 335 km. How much further does Isla have to travel?

Bar model

Number line

Number sentence

Isla is setting out cups and saucers at a school fair. She has 265 cups but only 232 saucers. How many cups won't get a saucer?

Bar model

Number line

Number sentence

Turtle eggs are hatching on a beach. 479 eggs have already hatched. 189 eggs haven't hatched yet. How many eggs were laid to begin with?

Bar model

Number line

Number sentence

5

A decorator is hanging wallpaper. A roll of wallpaper is 355 cm long. This is too long for the wall so he cuts a piece off. The piece measures 117cm. How long is the wall?

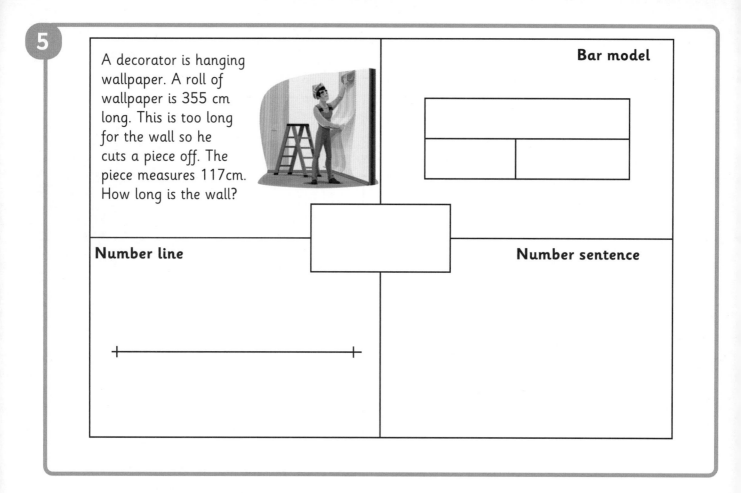

Bar model

Number line

Number sentence

★ Challenge

Complete this Think Board. You will need to think of your own question!

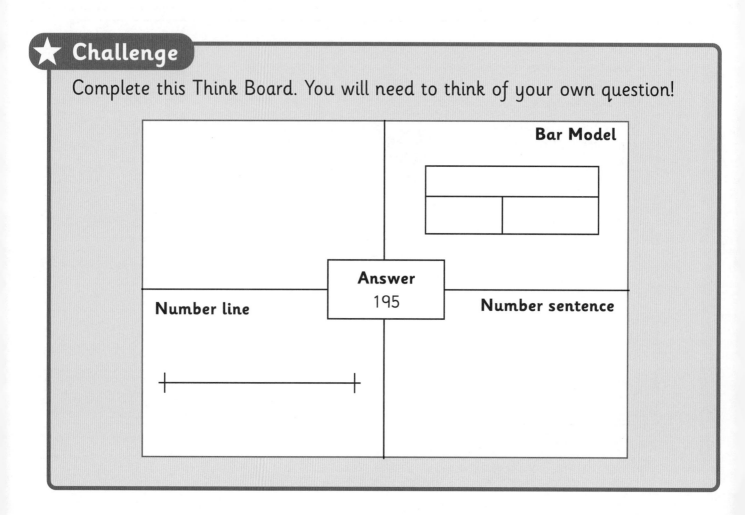

Bar Model

Answer
195

Number line

Number sentence

3.15 Two-step word problems

Solve these two-step word problems.

Choose the strategies you feel most confident with. You could draw a bar model.

1 Amman collects football cards. He has 230 of them. On his birthday, he is given another 170 cards. He puts half of his cards in an album and takes the other half to school. How many cards does he take to school?

2 A school carries out a survey of 450 children to find out how they travel to school. 278 children walk to school, 107 go by bus and 18 cycle to school. Everyone else goes by car. How many children travel to school by car?

3 Isla is making decorations for a school fair. She looks in her mum's sewing box and finds 87 cm of pink ribbon, 284 cm of blue ribbon, and some red ribbon. The red ribbon is 120 cm shorter than the blue ribbon. How much ribbon does Isla have?

Pink ribbon	87 cm
Blue ribbon	284 cm
Red ribbon	

Total ribbon =

4 A theatre has 900 seats. 339 adults and some children go to the theatre for a show and sit down. There are 69 empty seats. How many children are sitting in the theatre?

5 In Isla's fridge, there are 144 grapes and some cherries. Isla eats half the cherries, and there are now 220 pieces of fruit in the fridge. How many cherries were in the fridge to begin with?

6 In a school there are 219 boys, 225 girls and the teachers. If there are 489 people in the school, how many are teachers?

7 The children are guessing the number of sweets in a jar. Amman guesses there are 189 sweets. Finlay's guess is 16 less than Amman's and 25 more than Nuria's. What were Finlay and Nuria's guesses?

8 A woman has to travel 522 km for work. She travels 368 km by plane and 145 km by train. She takes a taxi for the final part of the journey. How far does she travel by taxi?

9 A farm has sheep, cows and pigs. There are 200 cows and 122 pigs. The number of sheep is double the number of pigs. How many animals are there on the farm?

★ **Challenge**

Write your own two-step question. Decide on the numbers you will use first, by completing this bar model:

4.1 Dividing by skip counting

1 Finlay is putting apples into boxes. Skip count to work out how many apples are in each box. Draw the skips on the number lines.

Write a division sentence to show your answer.

a) 16 apples in two boxes

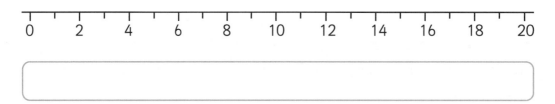

b) 16 apples in four boxes

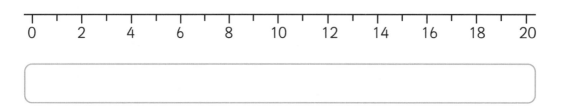

c) 35 apples in five boxes

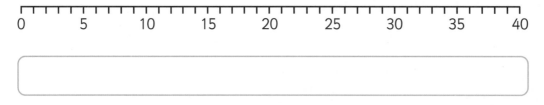

d) 15 apples in three boxes

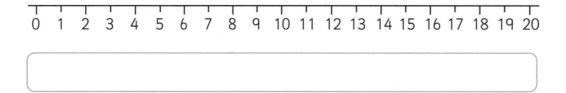

2 Thirty children are playing a game. When the teacher calls a number, the children go into groups of that number.

For each number, skip count to work out how many groups there are.

Write a division sentence for each answer.

a) 3 children in a group ⬚ groups ⬚

b) 6 children in a group ⬚ groups ⬚

c) 5 children in a group ⬚ groups ⬚

3 Skip count to solve each division. Use the number line to help you.

a) 24 ÷ 2 = ⬚   b) 25 ÷ 5 = ⬚

c) 18 ÷ 3 = ⬚   d) 24 ÷ 4 = ⬚

★ Challenge

Finlay is working out how many groups of 10 there are in 50. He draws this diagram.

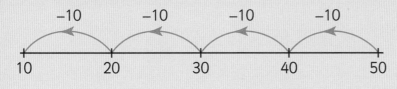

Finlay says, "There are 4 groups of 10." Is he correct? Explain your thinking.

4.2 Dividing with remainders

1 For each problem, circle **yes** or **no** to say if there will be any left over. Then write how many are left over.

a) 23 strawberries shared between 5 children.

yes **no** [   ] are left over.

b) 40 blueberries shared between 5 children.

yes **no** [   ] are left over.

c) 15 apples shared between 3 children.

yes **no** [   ] are left over.

d) 14 pears shared between 3 children.

yes **no** [   ] are left over.

e) 13 bananas shared between 2 children.

yes **no** [   ] are left over.

f) 14 oranges shared between 3 children.

yes **no** [   ] are left over.

2 Finlay is putting flowers into vases. He has 19 flowers and must put 3 in each vase.

a) How many vases will he need?

b) How many flowers will be left over?

c) Write a division sentence to show your answer.

3 Work out these problems and record any remainders. One has been done for you.

a) 20 ÷ 3 = 6 r 2

b) 18 ÷ 3 =

c) 19 ÷ 3 =

d) 22 ÷ 2 =

e) 21 ÷ 2 =

f) 28 ÷ 5 =

g) 18 ÷ 5 =

A fairground ride allows 6 people in a cabin. If a class of 32 children all want to go on the ride, how many cabins must there be for them all to get on? Explain your thinking.

4.3 Solving multiplication problems

1 Use your knowledge of doubles to work out the answers to these problems. Draw an array to help you. Explain how you used doubles to work out each answer.

a) 9×4

b) 5×6

c) 3×8

2 Think about ways to solve these problems using facts you know.

Explain how you worked out each answer.

a) In a shop, marbles come in bags of 7. There are 4 bags on the shelf. How many marbles altogether?

b) The teacher asks Amman to put 5 pencils on every table. There are 8 tables in the classroom. How many pencils does he need?

c) In a library there are 7 display shelves. Each shelf has 5 books on it. How many books are on display?

d) Isla has invited 5 friends to tea. Her mum decides to give the 6 children 3 fish fingers each. How many fish fingers does her mum need to buy?

e) A florist has 6 vases. Each vase has 8 flowers in it. How many flowers are there altogether?

3 Look at this array.

Write a multiplication sentence for it and work out the answer.

a) Use your answer to work out the answer to 5 × 4.

b) Now write down the answer to 4 × 3.

★ Challenge

Without working out the answers, write <, >, or = to make the statements true. Explain your choice for each pair.

6 × 3 [ ] 8 × 4

2 × 12 [ ] 6 × 4

18 × 2 [ ] 9 × 3

14 × 8 [ ] 7 × 5

4.4 Multiplying by 100

1 For each problem, show what happens to the ones digit using the place value grid. Then write the answer. One has been done for you.

a) $3 \times 100 =$ 300

Hundreds	Tens	Ones
		3
3	0	0

b) $2 \times 100 =$ ___

Hundreds	Tens	Ones

c) $7 \times 100 =$ ___

Hundreds	Tens	Ones

d) $6 \times 100 =$ ___

Hundreds	Tens	Ones

2 Work out the missing numbers.

a) $100 \times \boxed{} = 800$

b) $\boxed{} \times 100 = 400$

c) $100 \times \boxed{} = 900$

d) $6 \times \boxed{} = 600$

e) $100 \times \boxed{} = 500$

f) $100 \times \boxed{} = 1000$

3 Amman's dad's car is 100 times as long as the picture of his car.

How long is Amman's dad's car?

Write the problem as a multiplication sentence and solve it.

←—4 cm—→

★ **Challenge**

Finlay has 8p. Isla has 10 times as much, and Nuria has 10 times as much as Isla. How much money does Nuria have? Write a multiplication sentence to show the problem and solve it.

If Amman has £80, how many times as much money does he have than Finlay's 8p? Show your working.

1 For each problem, show what happens to the ones digit using the place value grid. Then write the answer. One has been done for you.

a) $100 \div 100 = \boxed{1}$

Hundreds	Tens	Ones
1	0	0 → 1

b) $500 \div 100 = \boxed{}$

Hundreds	Tens	Ones

c) $800 \div 100 = \boxed{}$

Hundreds	Tens	Ones

d) $300 \div 100 = \boxed{}$

Hundreds	Tens	Ones

2 Work out the missing numbers.

a) $600 \div \boxed{} = 6$

b) $\boxed{} \div 100 = 5$

c) $\boxed{} \div 100 = 6$

d) $400 \div 100 = \boxed{}$

e) $200 \div \boxed{} = 2$

f) $\boxed{} \div 100 = 10$

3 A real elephant is 300 cm tall.

Amman draws a picture of an elephant that is exactly 100 times smaller than a real elephant.

How tall is Amman's picture?

Write the problem as a division sentence and solve it.

★ Challenge

A number divided by 10 then by 10 again gives 4 tens and 38 ones.

Isla thinks the calculation must be 78000 ÷ 10 ÷ 10 = 78.

Is she correct? Explain your answer.

1 Write a multiplication sentence and a division sentence for each array. One has been done for you.

a)

$$3 \times 4 = 12$$
$$12 \div 3 = 4$$

b)

2 Reverse these division sentences to turn them into multiplication sentences. Write the multiplication sentence.

a) $18 \div 6 = 3$

b) $24 \div 6 = 4$

c) $21 \div 3 = 7$

d) $35 \div 5 = 7$

e) $90 \div 10 = 9$

3 Isla is putting chairs out for assembly. There are 50 chairs and she needs to put them into 5 rows. How many chairs does she put in each row?

Write a multiplication sentence and a division sentence to show the answer.

4 There are 35 cars in a car park. Each row of parking spaces has 5 cars in it. How many rows of parking spaces are there?

Write a multiplication sentence and a division sentence to show the answer.

The children are working on missing number problems.

Nuria says $12 \div \boxed{} = 4$ is the same as $\boxed{} \div 4 = 12$.

Is she correct? Explain your thinking.

4.7 Recalling multiplication and division facts for 2, 5 and 10

1 Use your knowledge of multiplication facts for 2, 5 and 10 to answer these questions.

a) 4 lots of 5 are ☐

b) 10 × 3 = ☐

c) 6 groups of 2 are ☐

d) 2 × 8 = ☐

e) 2 lots of 5 are ☐

f) 6 × 10 = ☐

2 Use your knowledge of multiplication facts to find the missing number.

a)
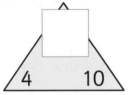

b)
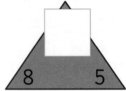

c)
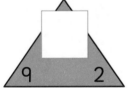

d)
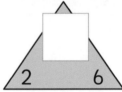

e)
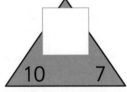

f)
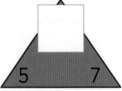

3 Use your knowledge of multiplication and division facts to write a multiplication sentence and a division sentence for each triangle.

a)
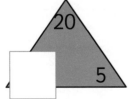

b)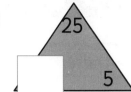

c)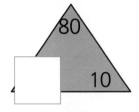

d)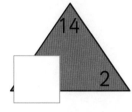

4

a) $10 \times \boxed{} = 120$

b) $\boxed{} \div 2 = 8$

c) $40 \div \boxed{} = 5$

d) $\boxed{} \times 10 = 70$

e) $45 \div \boxed{} = 5$

f) $\boxed{} \div 5 = 7$

★ Challenge

Amman has made this number triangle.

What could the missing numbers be? Make a list of all the possibilities.

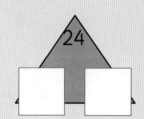

Now write multiplication and division facts for each number. How many different multiplication and division facts can you write?

4.8 Multiplying and dividing using known facts

1 Use your knowledge of multiplying by 10 and 100 to solve these problems.

a) 40 × 10 = ☐

b) 40 × 20 = ☐

c) 400 × 2 = ☐

d) 200 × 4 = ☐

e) 300 × 2 = ☐

f) 30 × 20 = ☐

2 Amman is ordering a jotter for every child in a school.

- Jotters come in boxes of 100.
- There are 782 children in the school.

I should order 7 boxes.

You should order 8 boxes.

Who is right? Explain your thinking.

☐

3 Use your knowledge of dividing by 10 and 100 to solve these problems.

a) 40 ÷ 2 = [ ]

b) 40 ÷ 4 = [ ]

c) 80 ÷ 4 = [ ]

d) 800 ÷ 10 = [ ]

e) 800 ÷ 20 = [ ]

f) 600 ÷ 3 = [ ]

g) 1000 ÷ 10 = [ ]

h) 1000 ÷ 100 = [ ]

4 In a factory, robots packs boxes with pencils.

Write a multiplication sentence or a division sentence for each question and answer it.

a) Robot A packs boxes with 10 pencils. How many boxes are needed for 500 pencils?

b) Robot B packs boxes with 20 pencils. How many boxes are needed for 600 pencils?

c) Robot C has filled 40 boxes with 20 pencils in each. How many pencils did it pack?

5 A farmer is packing eggs into boxes. Each box can hold 20 eggs. How many boxes are needed for these numbers of eggs?

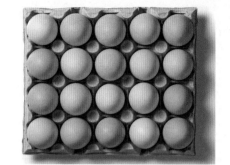

a) 400 eggs ☐   b) 80 eggs ☐

c) 240 eggs ☐   d) 180 eggs ☐

★ **Challenge**

The children have been playing a game.

Nuria scored 3 times as many points as Amman.

Amman scored twice as many points as Isla.

Isla scored 10 times as many points as Finlay.

Nuria scored 900 points. What did the other children score?

Complete the table.

Nuria	Amman	Isla	Finlay
900			

4.9 Solving number problems

1 Marbles come in bags of 10. Amman buys 5 bags of marbles and Isla buys 8 bags of marbles.

Show how you worked out each part of the problem.

How many marbles does Amman have?

How many marbles does Isla have?

How many more marbles does Isla have?

2 Nuria is taking part in a skating competition.

- There are 5 judges.

- Each judge gives Nuria the same score.

If her points total is 35, how many points did each judge give? Show how you worked out your answer.

3. In a pet shop, mice cost £4 and fish cost £3. How much would it cost altogether for:

Show how you worked out each part of the problem.

a) 5 mice and 4 fish

b) 3 mice and 10 fish

c) 2 mice and 5 fish

d) Is it cheaper to buy 2 mice and 5 fish or 4 mice and 2 fish? Explain your thinking.

4. Finlay is planting bulbs.

He has 25 daffodil bulbs and plants them in rows of 5. He has 12 crocus bulbs and plants them in rows of 6. How many rows of flowers does he plant altogether? Show how you worked out the answer.

Entrance to the amusement park costs £10 for an adult and £5 for a child. A family ticket for 2 adults and 2 children costs £25.

Finlay's going with his family and some friends. There are 5 adults and 7 children.

What is the cheapest way for them all to enter the park?

Show your working.